HUE & CRY

Diane K. Martin

MadHat Press
Cheshire, Massachusetts

MadHat Press
PO Box 422, Cheshire MA 01225

Copyright © 2020 Diane K. Martin
All rights reserved

The Library of Congress has assigned
this edition a Control Number of
2020932967

ISBN 978-1-941196-98-4 (paperback)

Cover design by Marc Vincenz
Cover image: *Head of a Woman,* Pablo Picasso, 1908
Author photo by John F. Martin
Book design by MadHat Press

www.MadHat-Press.com

Table of Contents

I

In the Mouth of the Wolf	3
Refract	4
Angle of Incidence	5
Muse's Warning	6
Bomb	7
Earthquake Weather	8
Silent Night	10
Fernande Olivier: *Femme dormante (meditation)*, 1904	11
Gertrude Stein: *Portrait de Gertrude Stein*, 1906	14
Eva Gouel (Marcelle Humbert): *Ma jolie*, 1912	16
A Study in Chiaroscuro	18
Self-Help Dream of the Yellow Canvas	19

II

Piece of Work	23
Plot	24
POV	25
MacGuffin	26
Radio Frequency	27
Beatles on Acid	28
Cold Music	30
Bird Through Frames	32
Morse: Notes for the Final Episode	33
[The awkward angle of the angel's hand]	34
Red Herring	35
Jigsaw	36
Excusez-moi de vous déranger	37

One Question   38
Gabrielle Lespinasse: *Gaby mon amour, mon ange,*
   1916   39
Irène Lagut: *La femme assise,* 1917   40
Olga Koklova: *Portrait d'Olga dans un fauteuil,* 1918   41

III

Hue and Cry   45
The Party   48
La Vie (en Rose)   49
Shocking the Well   51
Evening Light   52
Night Mind   53
Indelible   54
At the Origin of the World   55
Jesus in Paris   57
Fata Morgana   59
Penelope Tessitura   60
Marie-Thérèse Walter: *Le rêve,* 1932   61
Dora Maar: *Femme en pleurs,* 1937   63
Françoise Gilot: *La femme-fleur,* 1946   65

IV

Bag Lady's Song   70
Magpie Beauty   71
Grace   72
West County Metaphors   73
What It Takes   74
They Come   76
Life Drawing   77
Ars Poetica   78
Soleil Levant: Zabriskie Point   79

Geneviève Laporte: *Le soleil ébloui*, 1951	80
Sylvette David: *Portrait de Sylvette*, 1954	81
Jacqueline Roque: *Femme nue au bonnet turc*, 1955	82
Muse Rebellion	83
What She Meant	85
Will's Will	86
Gertrude Said Matisse's Pears	87
Take 5	88
Shutting the Door	89
Notes	91
Acknowledgments	93
About the Author	97

Vissi d'arte, vissi d'amore
—aria from *Tosca,* Giacomo Puccini

*The blue light was my baby
and the red light was my mind.*
—"Love in Vain," Robert Johnson

I

In the Mouth of the Wolf

> *Everyone has a great, horrible opera inside him ...*
> —Sarah Ruhl, playwright
> *... [There are] different kinds of dire*
> —Rebecca Solnit

Stradella sang *We leave tomorrow, are you willing?*
but Cornélie Falcon could not answer—the wolf

spat *I no longer have a future* from the soprano's mouth.
Yes, there are different kinds of dire. A retriever is found

alive after eight days in quake rubble, no human left,
house razed. (Note: the dire wolf, preserved in La Brea tar,

larger and fiercer than ancestors of our Bella—bones
of birds and ruminating beasts in what was its belly.)

The three-year-old in the orphanage would not stop crying.
Her father did not remember where he left her.

A debris-covered sofa faced the television. A man
raised his arms in prayer. A boy walked his bike.

Diane K. Martin

Refract

If human life moves from matter to spirit, fact to story,
is it more than the breeze shot through aspens,
turning its gold medallions?
                Light waves pass
through a glass and move at a different pace
in the watery medium.
                As she is, not what she will be—
girl in the too-big coat on the train, who sings
eensy-weensy spider to her fingers—
                What a hurry we are in to lift off
into silkscreens of memory! Dante the car jockey pines
for the boom of the nineties:
                Those days, sometimes forty cars
would stack up at the curb. And still cigar smoke drifts
on the Embarcadero
                under an emoticon moon.

Angle of Incidence

The windows on the long side of the railroad flat
looked out across the airshaft to those of the next
door apartment. Once she found him sitting in

the dark waiting for something to start, as if what
happened in that theater was real and all the rest—
grocery bags on the wooden floor, mail unopened

on the sofa—was not. He gestured to her as a hand,
braceleted and slender, raised a white muslin shade
with the circle pull, then set out candles and silver

for dinner. And she got down beside him, traveling
her hand up the inseam of his pants and unbuttoning
her blouse—he, watching the other side of the glass,

and she imagining the neighbors across the way—
unaware of what her dark world concealed, a woman
on her knees, long hair down her naked back.

Diane K. Martin

Muse's Warning

You draw aside the curtains and you think
daylight has vanquished all vestiges,

but I am the comb you pull through your hair,
the keen and perilous razor. Your coffee

tastes of me, hot and bitter. The clothes
that you wear mask a carapace scarred

by words used as weapons. I am not
to blame for rough seas, bad weather. You

beg for amnesty, time, divine dispensation.
You didn't mean to go this far, or maybe

you thought the star you were born under
would always be lucky. Trust me, it isn't.

Bomb

This is a novel about the bomb plot
narrowly averted. Don't fret; it's short.
      Screenplay, you say? but how

portray the protagonist's pangs, second
thoughts? Flashback to his mother's labor,
      childhood taunts for his stammer

or his stature or his second-hand shoes.
Pan to his little girl in the playground.
      That's enough. This is the script

about the bomb defused—not the fire,
not the flames, blue and brighter, not the metal
      molten, not the screams, the shards,

the lightning. You can almost smell
burnt hair, blood's tang, flesh roasting. But this
      is not about the pyre. In this one,

your terrorist sleeps in. The six-year-old, brow
furrowed, concentrates on jacks; her terrier
      licks his privates beside her. She hums

a tune she just made up. Tonight her papa will
cook their supper. Her mama touches her brush
      tip to her lip, then to her paints.

Diane K. Martin

Earthquake Weather

She sees Rick in everything:
the child's ears, a robin,
television.

It was her gun he used,
but his car she found
him in.

Wind brought charred
headlines, instructions
for a VCR.

His was a breech birth,
born upside down and
topsy-turvy.

He loved swings, round-
abouts, whatever made
him dizzy.

He almost did it then, but
the gun did not work
for him.

They sat together on the
hill, waiting for more
aftershocks.

Not his fault, but the
rift between them
widened.

Some said he had a knife,
others, he would
never.

There were signs: animal
cries, dead birds, wind,
temblors.

Or it could have been
this; the child is
not telling.

Diane K. Martin

Silent Night

She grieved for the two-dimensional frog sculpted
        into its asphalt shadow; she ached
considering the fate of the pollarded planes. Each
        rag animal and headless doll required
a parting gesture before she laid herself down with
        herself, her breath a labored song.
Sometimes she slept between mattress and wall,
        sometimes on the cool wood floor naked
with the silverfish, or she would sit in the street
        with her flute, then return to the dark
living room to play the songs she knew on the piano
        —Beatles tunes and a Christmas medley:
"Joy to the World," "Good King Wenceslas," "Silent Night."

Fernande Olivier: *Femme dormante (meditation)*, 1904

I detest Sundays. I tell you, they smell bad.
That Sunday I lay in bed with a book, thinking
only of that first night with Pablo—how
the wind took the trees in Place Ravignan,
how the rain soaked my blouse to the skin.
But Pablo blocked my way in. I'd seen him
around le Bateau-Lavoir, of course, that Andalusian
the artists and poets all followed. (One night,
they marched drunk, shouting: *Up with Verlaine!
Down with Laforgue!* Or was it the other way round?
No matter.) Well, there he stood in the doorway,
holding the smallest wet kitten. *Voici Minou,* he laughed,
she is as wet as you. Then he invited me in to see
his new etching—you know the one I mean
—two blue people, blue wine, piece of blue bread
scratched in zinc with a hatpin from the floor
of a brothel. Pablo, Pablo, face so old,
eyes, coal hardened to diamonds. His hands,
delicate as a girl's, removed my wet hat,
my shoes, my stockings, slowly, and my lace....

On that muggy Sunday I lay in bed, the air so close,
it didn't seem I could stir of my own volition
—more like the Fates pushed me to leave Laurent
for good. I packed my things into Pablo's trunk,
got him to drag it down the hall to his place. *Mon Dieu,*

the smell! It seems his pal Apollinaire had the bright idea
to clean the floor with paraffin, then with bleach to rid
the place of paraffin, then eau de cologne, which stank to hell.

There I stayed seven years, as much a part of his studio
as the mattress propped on tins, the iron stove,
the yellow bowl. We lived for Beauty and Experience—
we smoked opium and stared into the flame of dreams
with the other *artistes*. We had nothing to do
with *les petits bourgeois* farts who lived in the classy
parts of town. Weekends we might buy Pablo a shirt
at the open-air market for a couple of centimes. In winter,
tea left in a cup was ice by morning. Summer found Pablo
painting shirtless in the heat, scarf around his waist.
Some days we ate only macaroni or dined on credit in cafés,
running up bills so high, they let us in only as hope
of payment. Once we were so hungry we cooked and ate
a sausage Minou found. But sometimes a dealer came
and left enough for wine, and Pablo would buy me
lavender *parfum* in cut-glass *bouteilles*.

Oui, certainement, he loved me, or the idea of me,
or the idea of love. You can see this portrait:
he watches while I sleep. Day after day, I lay
behind a curtain while he painted and held court.
He said he would starve for me. (But what I had to do
to get him to wash!) He enshrined my hat
as if it were a holy relic. He forbade me model

or even shop or clean. So I slept and read,
une femme décorative, as Gertrude called me.
With me in his life, he left behind brothels
and blue canvases. Rose hues bloomed,
saltimbanques began their strolls. Still,
he was a man who gnawed his own bones;
all he ever thought about was painting,
though doing it did not make him happy. And
there was no asking, *Pablo, what is the matter?*

                        As for me, I get bored.
If I'd been a man, I could have lived by my skills.
I hated being locked in (like the white mouse
he kept in a drawer), while one girl or another
au Lapin Agile sat laughing in his lap. And so
I never really meant to leave, but when I did,
could not find my way back.

Diane K. Martin

Gertrude Stein: *Portrait de Gertrude Stein,* 1906

I am I because my little dog knows me.
—Gertrude Stein

It happened Sunday afternoons at 27 rue de Fleurus in verbal duels with Matisse yes Cubism yes I put their pictures on my walls that first museum of modern art before it happened on their canvasses I am the genius who seated them across from their paintings.

My genius was seeing Picasso's genius and writing it and making him what he was but what he was was painting. The child he was was drawing while others did ABCs and when he grew he was emptying himself in painting what he had to say he was saying in painting.

Picasso was painting faces and hands and bodies not concerning himself with souls but seeing with the mind seeing a complete idea in his brain the way Galileo proved his telescope could see objects the eyes could not that were there were the moons of Jupiter.

Eighty times I climbed that Montmartre hill and down into Bateau Lavoir and sat as he was painting me then painting it out but in those Cubist hills of Gósol he could see me not looking at me or like me but he said it would be me and now this is Gertrude Stein for me.

At the end of the war walking at night in Paris together we saw trucks in camouflage a new thing we were seeing yes he

said to me that is Cubism we are seeing we made that and
then the world was seeing but Picasso had already seen it he
was painting then something else.

Diane K. Martin

Eva Gouel (Marcelle Humbert): *Ma Jolie,* 1912

C'est moi in that painting called *Ma Jolie*
(though I don't know how one can see
anyone's pretty thing in all those planes
of Cubism). Those evenings at *l'Ermitage,*
people stared at us four, *la belle Fernande*
next to bird-boned me. What a picture!

But Fernande longed for pursuit, thought
she'd have a go of it when young Ubaldo
wooed her. She knew there was no future
with that Futurist—it was just a game to her
to get Pablo jealous, and I, well, I'm not sure
what she wanted of me, a decoy dance maybe

to distract Pablo? Ah, but it worked too well!
He was only too glad to be rid of her. Once
he found a home for the dog, Frika, well
Fernande, *elle a disparu.* With one sure stroke
(the way they say the young Pablo would draw
a donkey with one line from the foot when

dared by other children)—*alors,* he erased
Fernande and crowned me first woman, Eva.
Je crois he lost his taste for *le bifteck,* and now
he savored quail; I let him crunch my bones
without squawk or cheep. *Ça ne fait rien.*
The world has fractured, fallen apart.

Pablo painted reality, not *réalisme*. I took care
of him—made dinner, sent Kahnweiler his
invoices. No more dog turds on the floor,
no piles of ashes in the chimney. Did Pablo
say that life was not to be spent with any one
woman? *Mais, souvenez-vous bien,* he did not

leave me; it was the cancer that took me. How
frightened he was of *la mort,* Pablito, as if he'd
met it before. Yes, he was the bull in the ring,
fierce but standing no chance once pierced by
the picadors. And the vapors floated from the
cemetery, the ghost of Casagemas at the window.

Diane K. Martin

A Study in Chiaroscuro

Sometimes what feels good is the most dangerous.
Remember uncle sun staring at your décolletage.
Think the daintiest little bright mushrooms.
Whose fault is it if you won't listen, if you
indulge too easily the heart's clamor?

Inside a small screen, brown Bakelite exterior,
a cathode ray soul screams at each scuffle
closer to the goal line. Beyond, schoolmates
in penny loafers and knee socks shuffle down leafy
sidewalks, pressing loose leaf binders to the chest.

From the pellucid moment of this autumn morning,
you still can't change the channel. You want to turn
blind eyes to that escapade—and to the airport angel
with her well-worn harp—could you afford to give
her absolution, say, an E-for-effort blessing?

If there were a God, do you think He would be
the red-shouldered hawk sheltering the fledgling,
or the fierce raptor seizing the gopher, greedy and slow,
clambering to its burrow? Shouldn't the gopher have
been warned by the shadow of the wings overhead?

Self-Help Dream of the Yellow Canvas

She'd never worked in oils, but she pictured
the canvas luscious and slick, an oily yolk
of glorious yellow, a radiant swath
of luxurious gold. The surface measured
two meters square, and she covered it
with even, horizontal strokes, using
a wide brush to diffuse the viscosity,
spreading the butter to morning.
She kept looking down at her hands,
the flecks of sunlight under her nails.
The path she took was transformed.

II

Piece of Work

The night is almost too quiet.
His snore is the exhaust of a semi
roaring down the two-lane. The dog

at her water bowl is a summer lake
lapping the silt beach. And the woman
—big glasses, denim jeans, hair

pulled back with a scarf—holds
a yellow pencil in her teeth.
The woman is the poem.

Diane K. Martin

Plot

You already know what happens
between breakfast and dinner, city
and country, birth and death—
and the hero, his height, weight,
neglected childhood, twilight gray
eyes, and predilection for lying.
A storm blows in from the west,
neighbors wheel in their trash bins,
fog mutes the traffic on the freeway.
Can you smell the coming rain,
the spice of the clove currant, the gin
of the juniper? *The heir to the troubles
is not born yet. The fixing of swords
is a commonplace of magic. Out,
damn'd spot. Watson, come! The game
is afoot.* Snails drown in a half inch
of Budweiser. The gopher tugs the tulip
bulb to its burrow. Fish in deep pools
swim in circles, waiting for a hook.

POV

Although not for whatever lay dead in the adjacent meadow,
for us the moment was perfect—the sky, sky blue, the sun
burnishing the fresh-washed foliage, the dog, sticks retrieved,

content to lie within reach of a scratch, and the narrative
permitting us a bench and a view of what lay before us:
the light green nap of grass like a billiard table's baize cloth,

turkey vultures cruising on the thermals in slow circles,
their shadows darkening tender shoots as they descend
first to perch on the fence and then to take their turns.

Diane K. Martin

MacGuffin

Thingamajig, gizmo, doohickey, gadget: useful
for trapping lions in the Scottish Highlands
where there are no lions to be trapped, that
thing that keeps the movie going, drives the plot
—Maltese Falcon, Holy Grail—that makes you
turn the page or stay up past bedtime—invented
by Hitchcock who certainly used it, though it's
said he took the term from a Scottish friend.
Think of that coin, *objet,* holy relic, jewel that
anyone would die for—maybe your crescent
and star, your star of David, or your cross.

Radio Frequency

Oyster white and loaf shaped, the radio
held boys singing around a tiny mic

though how transported from station
to station didn't figure into her equation.

Their joyous voices drowned out jokes:
My daddy lies over my mommy, and that's

what happened to me, mewled Butch,
from row three, then threw acorns

and called her *witch.* Time elapsed
and the meaning of words scratched

in bathroom stalls became evident,
but *O say* those harmonies evoked

a different key. When *Playboy* revealed
those boys were men, she sobbed

into her pillow at twilight's last gleaming;
the dawn's early light showed proof

their chords were still streaming, so
proudly she hailed, gallantly they waved.

Diane K. Martin

Beatles on Acid

You've heard the anecdote about
the first time the mop-tops dropped
the LSD that George's dentist slipped

into their rum and cokes? Admit:
It's not the acid that shocks but
the vision of George reclining

whilst this dentist bloke pokes his gums
and teeth and asks him if he flossed.
Yes, JFK bonked Marilyn, but when

Mailer met Her Blondeness she
was babushka'd, nose swollen
and red from a cold. What if she'd

had the chutzpah to grow old
before taking her exit? We don't want
to know that Julia Roberts' skin

is pearlescent by dint of Photoshop,
that Princess Diana barfed up dinner
so she wouldn't get fat, that Tony Curtis

was born Bernie Schwartz, or that
Helmut Newton's stylist applied lapis
shadow to Elizabeth Taylor's eyelids

to bring out the pool's chlorine blue
and the diamonds' sparkle. Couldn't
the gods just stay put on Olympus?

Diane K. Martin

Cold Music

> ... *it's been down there dreaming of being a violin*
> —Peter Van Arsdale, violin maker

1650: European winters are long and cold,
summers short and cool, and a woman
mumbles to herself, wool-clad mornings
in the kitchen garden—would there be enough
beetroot and barley to get them through?
Perhaps next year would be warmer.
The Alpine spruce she gathers from the forest floor
burns with blue-white heat. But when chartered
woodsmen send the hard, dense lumber
down the Po to brine in the Adriatic,
Antonio Stradivari finds it prime to craft
an instrument whose vibrato shimmers
with blue-white heat. Did this soak allow
the wood to absorb apothecary herbs
the luthier used to ward off worms and rot?
Is the glue that holds the instrument together
the key to its flawless tone, or the tender way
he sculpted belly to the back? Was it the metric
Stradivari used to indicate where to carve
f-hole eyes according to the Golden Ratio?
Or the practice of crushing gems and glass
to coat the instrument with a brittle lacquer?
Bows made from tail hairs of Mongolian stallions?
Or mere serendipity, accident of coldest weather,
something they can't duplicate or measure,

that Stradivari could feel in the violin when
he tucked the instrument under his chin?

Diane K. Martin

Bird Through Frames

Framed by the window, a raven
soars and sweeps in hale November.

The piano's andante moderato creates
another frame. We watch, expecting

the bird to land on the English holly,
gravid with berries. But it circles

the tree, opens out to a spiral, flips,
and comes around for another pass.

The piece shifts into allegro, the raven whips
and slides, and when the music turns

again—meno mosso—the raven dips
back to stately ritardando.

Piano silences. We return to chores,
the bird to its own music.

Morse: Notes for the Final Episode

Detective Chief Inspector Morse was just returning from the loo and set to order another pint when he saw her, back from the outback and bedecked with jewels—big heavy things, amber and as large as apricots. *This one's on me,* she said, by way of demonstrating that she'd earned a top degree and had more than the necessary to pay for it. Then she reached into her bra, retrieved a pitch pipe, and raised her lovely arms, whereupon the jewelry clanged and jangled, and the orchestra joined her in the aria *Vissi d'arte, vissi d'amore,* "I lived for art, I lived for love," from Tosca by Puccini. So it was that Morse knew where he'd ended.

Diane K. Martin

[The awkward angle of the angel's hand]

The awkward angle
of the angel's hand
holding the trumpet,
the curtain's fluid ascent,
a plaster foot plunging
through the cloud ceiling,
and the minute variation in
cherubim lantern ignition
—opera from the second row
an earthly creation, however
approximating heaven.

Red Herring

Motives: everyone's got one—bully boss, sibling rival, business partner absconding with the funds: trespass, treason, spousal *in flagrante*. But do you think you could swing the lead pipe in the library, wield the candlestick in the kitchen, stab, stab, stab, with the dagger in the hall? It takes a special talent to murder. Consider, Wile E. Coyote aside, there's no backsies, and there's all that mess of a corpse. Yes, perhaps you've got a problem with the property line and the pissant neighbor who's had one too many one too many times. But even the hypothetically culpable aren't necessarily capable—just over-brined kippers designed to throw off the scent for the hounds.

Diane K. Martin

Jigsaw

—after Andrew O. Dugas

One large missing piece, a negative-shaped lizard,
climbed the stone wall with the bougainvillea,
the house and gardens in the jigsaw quaint, old
mortared stone, not up to code for California.
Each time, as she waited for her treatment, she
sorted through for that piece, as if it and its
completion on the viney wall held some significance,
but then at last she left the puzzle incomplete, saying,
let someone else finish it, someone who'll be
finished someday with what she was waiting for.

Excusez-moi de vous déranger

> For beauty is nothing but the beginning of terror …
> —Rilke

A light breeze ruffles the bougainvillea
and a takeout flyer rubber banded

to the gate. We swim hand in hand
through syrup air. Sweet alyssum.

Though grass is green under a sky-
blue tent, babes in arms coo, and over-

come canines bask in napped luxury,
there's a rent in the fabric, that perfect

cerulean, and hot winds from the abyss
issue through. It's not just me—the world

as you know it no longer fits. The dog
hears, halts, whimpers. The infant cannot

be consoled. You would weep if you could.
Can we close the bedroom door

and with our lips dispel it? Or inhale it
into alveoli where it will stain the blood?

Diane K. Martin

One Question

Would you love me more, if, let's say, my eyes
were chestnut? If I could whistle like a boy—
the neighbor boy—calling his dog, his mother's
bell clanging at dusk to summon him to supper?
What if I spoke with an accent, a grind of black
pepper? If I told lies, would you prosecute?
If I stole one scent every day from the banks
of the Seine? What if I ran out of emotion and
stood still? If my inertia overtook my gravity?
If we woke up together and no longer knew
each other, and I introduced myself as the villain
with the moustache demanding *the rent the rent*
from the girl with hair like a whitewater river?

Gabrielle Lespinasse: *Gaby mon amour, mon ange,* 1916

These words he inscribed on the painting
of our bed in moonlight. But I'm not surprised

you've not heard of me. He said he wanted
my mind to be free, he didn't want me to be sad.

No doubt he was feeling bad with his Eva dying.
So I gave comfort to the enemy—my boyfriend's

client, if you want to know. If Pablo asked me
to marry him, he had no ring and knew

the answer would be no and never quite
got around to introducing me to the renowned

Gertrude-and-Alice lionesses, who may not have
approved of his days by Eva's deathbed in Auteuil

and nights in my love nest on Boulevard Raspail.
I never asked for anything and never got it either.

Diane K. Martin

Irène Lagut: *La femme assise*, 1917

Yes, most likely he had me
in oils that he painted over
when he could not make me
his—although some say that's
my reluctance (and his truculence)
depicted in *The Lovers*. So this
pencil and crayon sketch will
have to do for you to know me.
But it was 1917, remember: Eva,
his father, his dog, *tout le monde*
was full of dying. He wanted
somebody—some body—
so badly he took me, kidnapped
and kept me under lock and key
in his house in Montrouge. But he
could not pin down *mon esprit*
nor my body, which escaped
through unlocked shutters.
You see, I had my own tale
to live (read Apollinaire's
La Femme Assise). And it was true,
what Pablo accused: I prefer to
share the smoke in bed with a woman.
So, I wasn't moved by his grief, pleas,
blackmail, force, or cajoling. He
didn't mark his territory on me.

Olga Koklova: *Portrait d'Olga dans un fauteuil,* 1918

You will not easily dismiss me. Oh, I know
they say Diaghilev only let me dance because
of the colonel, my father. But did Papa persuade
Picasso to pick me out of all the company dancers?
It is true what Sergei said: A Russian girl does not
simply fall for a fellow who makes sweet promises.
Pablo would have to court me, yes, and marry me
—twice, and in church, moreover. Well, *tant pis,*
perhaps, he got more than he bargained for.

You see me in this portrait—formal, not abstract.
I insist on recognizing my features. Though
what do I really care for art? They were *my*
well-placed friends who bought his paintings.
His suits I had made in London (though he
would wear the red bullfighter's sash with his
dinner jacket when we entertained the Count
and Countess de Beaumont). Those galas were
legendary! Yes, one evening Coco Chanel arrived

bronzed from the slopes; from then on
fashionable ladies devoted themselves to the
perfection of the tan. If Pablo provided for
the mahogany and lace that graced our flat on
rue La Boétie, I did my best to teach him manners,
but more and more he stayed upstairs—in his studio,

like the Montmartre hovel he shared with that whore,
Fernande. Perhaps I should have listened to Doña
Maria: *No woman could ever be happy with my son Pablo.*

I gave up the ballet because of my bum knee and baby
Paulo. Soon his father began to tire of painting Paulo's
latest stage, as if he were an old toy, to be cast aside for a
new one. To be cast aside! You probably think I curse
the day *la vache* Marie Thérèse came up from the Métro.
But if it weren't she, it would be some other silly Sally....
Yes, I despise Dora and Françoise, their nerve, their airs!
Even so, they come and go, but Spaniards do not divorce,
Alors, Pablo n'est pas français. I am forever Madame Picasso!

III

Hue and Cry

1.
The day seemed treacherous and wicked.
We hated breaking our promises.
We couldn't enter or exit.
We craved a way to be decent.
Elsewhere others went about their work.
We had done such a good job of distracting them.
As if faith brought redemption.
As if our terrors were visible.
At night no pattern was discernible in the heavens.
Moonless. Unconsecrated.
Imagine the first night of creation.
Haven't you ever wanted to be innocent?

2.
The day seemed unrelated to tomorrow or yesterday.
We hated the sound of our own names.
We couldn't imagine an ending.
We craved safety and order.
Elsewhere people had mothers, their mothers had children.
We had no hard feelings or soft sentiments.
As if a black hole was the center.
As if it all could vanish in one second.
At night you feel drawn to the infinite.
Moth-like. Magnetic.
Imagine finding a remedy.
Haven't you ever wanted to take the path of least resistance?

3.
The day seemed taut, curled in at the edges.
We hated being mistaken for tourists in our own country.
We couldn't go backward or forward.
We craved immunity from our reflections.
Elsewhere there were pools and reservoirs.
We had no memory of how we got here.
As if we were ants in an anthill.
As if there were gods on Olympus.
At night we woke and remembered.
The thaw. Renaissance.
Imagine green shoots on black earth.
Haven't you ever wanted to elude destiny?

4.
The day seemed a thin slice between two hard heels of night.
We hated to admit our pleasure.
We couldn't have stilled its birth.
We craved salt, but salt made us thirsty.
Elsewhere creatures were migrating.
We had no flock or feathers.
As if tomorrow brought winter.
As if winter would be a reckoning.
At night we were ready for anything.
Rampant. Wanton.
Imagine your fingers teaching you everything.
Haven't you ever wanted to escape the body's prison?

5.
The day seemed part of a vast string of days, unharnessed
    and unchanging.
We hated to think of the big picture.
We couldn't do anything but crawl on our bellies.
We craved landmarks, punctuation, percussive instruments.
Elsewhere, there were hurricanes, tornadoes.
We had to make do with what was given.
As if we were reading the last chapter.
As if we had to follow the author's bidding.
At night our dreams were untranslatable.
Effulgent. Magenta.
Imagine a wake transiting the ocean.
Haven't you ever wanted to walk on water?

Diane K. Martin

The Party

They tidy up, empty tortilla chips into the antique ceramic bowl she got from her mother, pour M&Ms into a cut glass dish. A rose petal falls, D minor bursts from a guitar. Yellow drapes make the whole room golden.

He stands in the kitchen, microbrew in hand, popping story after story like flies to the outfield. His hair is pomaded; shined are his shoes. His most inspired work is his epitaph, which he is constantly chiseling.

She wanders in, an old woman in a ravished country, scouring the landscape for kindling. She's the punch line to his joke, secret he can't divulge, shape-shifter, changeling. She tells of finding a kitten, her embouchure a meow-moue, her accent Castilian.

He skates uphill, hands at his back, on the blond carpet. Plates of shrimp swim past them. Above the sea of voices, cresting and breaking, a woman laughs. *Just look at you!*

Catalpa leaves flap like elephant ears.

La Vie (en Rose)

Sweet alyssum, she says, *smells like dog piss*—Army wife, married thirty-five years to a lifer, getting a divorce. But the pink panties in the Cécile Brünner are not evidence of illicit passion, just a rag the window cleaner lost.

Dark when you go out with the dog. The 7-Eleven twinkles in a wasted sky beside the flamingo pink Pentecostal church, once a movie theater. If it is Thursday, the Ford guy is shuttling his stable of Mustangs from one side of the street to the other. If it is Friday, he is moving them back.

When the phone rings, you are applying Aphrodite's Nightie pink polish to your toes. A man climbs out a basement window. He runs to a diner for coffee, the thick ceramic cup warming his hands. He leaves his hat under the counter when he calls you. The busboy finds the Borsalino and takes it home.

Valentine's day at the transit station: lacy pink-lettered ads, a profusion of pigeons. A woman draws a comb through long wet hair. By the time she gets to her stop, her hair has acquired a kind of permanence, like a baby shoe, bronzed.

In the daylight, you are blinded to the stars. You trust that they are out there: emerging, glowing pink, and dying white supernovas. Just as right this second someone is eating a tuna sandwich, someone is giving birth, someone is hammering a nail.

You face an A-frame barn, rusted cars and tall fennel in the foreground. You can see beyond, where rows of grapevines converge on a house. Inside is a bed, where three girls are sleeping—no, two are asleep; the oldest, turned to the wall, is peeling off wallpaper, a small pink square.

Shocking the Well

February. You ask if I am settling in.
Look: a shaft of sunlight. Call this picture
Woman in a Green Robe Reading a Well Report.
Think Vermeer:

*Bib at well head contaminated with coliform
greater than 6. CDHS recommends level 1.
Arsenic, nitrate: not detected.
Water moderately hard.*

We brush our teeth with bottled water.
We shock the well with chlorine.
After a day we turn on all faucets
and for hours flush the tap.

In the old house we could see
past the Farallones, all the way to China—
so we said, the vaulted ceiling extending
an infinite blur of sea and sky.

Now a pink plum blooms six feet from
our doorway. At night the tree exhales
trillions of stars, ones the ancients named,
connecting the dots to their lives.

Diane K. Martin

Evening Light:

They sit at the kitchen table. It's summer.
Overgrown shrubs partially frame the window.
Sunlight filters through the purple plum,
dazzling; she thinks of being underwater
with the kelp, schools of silver anchovies
swimming this way and that. He loves
the plush shadow, though the evening light
is clear and quenching, more liquid than at noon.
What was that bird? The neighbor said
when her dad died, they found a steno pad—
his life list—its name the last penciled note.

Night Mind

The night mind looks for someplace to land, suspended—
less the bloodthirsty mosquito or the hummingbird
hovering, wings beating eighty times per second,

than ghost—score unsettled, restless, volatile, afloat.
Perhaps, purblind and shackled, stumbling
over pea gravel and millennial tree stump, it seeks

the phantom limb, lost twin, coin in the snowdrift,
or attempts words of a prayer in the unwritten tongue
of a tribe now gone. For a while, it settles,

a palimpsest, scrubbing out and rewriting
old memories. When it looks forward, it finds
a wall of glass—no aerie for nesting, no toehold.

Diane K. Martin

Indelible

Ultramarine from lapis lazuli in Afghanistan
colors the robes of Titian's Virgin Marys
and the eyebrows on King Tut's death mask,

while resin from mummy wrappings makes
the pigment mummy brown. Red dragon's
blood from the rattan palm won't kill you,

but the arsenic in emerald green will. Carmine
extracted from cochineal beetles now pinks up
strawberry yoghurt, but once it demonstrated

Spanish power and gave British soldiers their
red coats. The pee from mango-leaf-eating cows
yields the rare and precious Indian yellow,

and tannin from oak galls the gall wasp vacates
makes an ochre pigment. You can find oak galls
in Aleppo or here in Sonoma. Mix tannin from

galls, gum arabic, and vinegar with iron from
two-penny nails—for ink, blackish purple and
indelible as my letter of undying love to you.

At the Origin of the World

after the painting by Gustave Courbet

He sits on a folding chair at the painting's left
for two and a half hours before the shift changes
but doesn't look at the larger-than-life legs
splayed on the white sheet, displaying pubis
and pudenda, and part of one naked breast,

an image so scandalous that more than one hundred
years passed from execution to exhibition. Like
a harem eunuch, he studies, instead, the visitors:
foreheads wrinkled in earnest contemplation,
the over-casual glance, affecting nonchalance,

faces, blushing or not—and then the few,
who, encountering the painting unprepared,
back out of the room. He has worked here
three years—give or take some sick days
last November and the August vacation—and still

in his dreams that torso looms. Perhaps it's the low
angle of the pose that creates the shock, the view
from below insisting on an intimacy greater
than the model's with what she owned—also that
like a corpse, she is unidentifiable, neither face

nor head visible. But no one makes trouble or tries
to get too close to the canvas. Indeed, these days,
you see more than just *réalisme*—nudes everywhere

online—and proud papas video their babies from the start. So much for genesis and genitals.

Jesus in Paris

Look, it was three days since she'd talked
to anyone, three days of fever and sleep,

sheets wet with sweat, though the January
wind banged the casements, with their cross-

hatched mullions. She could almost feel
someone in the room, though the concierge

sat six floors below, on guard, arms folded,
and the flatmate was at a Brussels conference

for young Christians. But the Bible the friend
left said Jesus would take her by the hand

if she believed in Him. Three days into that flu
the girl read chapter and verse full of thunder

and faith, acquiescence and begetting, sank
low with bones' and eyeballs' aching. She knew,

yea, she was dying! *Jesus,* she said then—aloud
so He could hear that she believed—oh how

she wanted to, and slept and woke to the Cross,
stark and indisputable on the plaster wall,

Diane K. Martin

wept and slept—and woke, fever gone,
curtains limp, moonlight dispelled by morning.

Fata Morgana

after Paul Klee's Fata Morgana zur See

Pastel pennants snap to a brisk tempo.
Curlicue clefs, fat violas, a lilt of masts
float in an apricot sky above the sketch
of craft, starboard in an assumption
of ocean. Let's suppose the boat: damp,
encrusted with salt-brittle barnacles.
The sailors, poor men, fond of rum,
charting a course between monster
and whirlpool, hear, skyward, a vibrato,
warble, and trill, and over the commotion,
the moans of thirst, despite the pitch
of the deck, behold the witch ship, rigged
and trimmed in splendor, and dazzled,
drift over the edge of the earth.

Diane K. Martin

Penelope Tessitura

You thought you could blend in with the forest, be
what the forest called for, solid as boulders that stay
where the glaciers put them. You keep the radio on

for ambience, fly down to Mexico to drown in long
vowels, trade your soul for sun-dappled surfaces.
You harvest grievances, swallow dreams whole

without chewing them, spend nights unweaving
what all day you wove, though you've lost the need
for cloth: its warmth, its weight, its color.

Marie-Thérèse Walter: *Le rêve,* 1932

            I took the Metro steps
two at a time and at top bumped into
a small middle-aged guy, forelock dangling
above eyes that held me fast. I didn't know
what to make of him. He said my face
would be all over his canvases
                 and let me go with a kiss
and a promise to return to him. Neither
who or what he was meant a thing to me.
I would have been far more impressed
with a top-scoring football forward or
a seeded player at Wimbledon.
                Mamam made me swear
to do as he said, since he was rich and famous.
I wonder if she knew in a few months' time,
her girl, who had kissed only her mama,
would spread her legs and raise her hips
above her shoulders for him.
                Oh my wonderful,
terrible lover. The funny things he made
me do! I'd never imagined such positions!
Sometimes I couldn't stop laughing—that
made him furious. But when I wept
he was pleased.
                His paintings don't
knock me out, and does this really look
like me? I never asked about his life.
He kept me across the street from his wife

and never lived with me. But he loved me,
I'm sure. Every day
            he loved me more, he said.
That odd woman, Dora, with the red nails,
should have gone. It was my place with him,
father of my baby. When our daughter
was born, he fell to his knees and named her
Maria de la Concepción
            after the baby sister
he had bartered with God to save. At thirteen,
he would have given up painting forever
if God had desired it. But his sister died
of diphtheria; so he went on painting
and gave up God instead.
            We called the baby Maya.
When Pablo was away, I'd close his room, tell her
she mustn't disturb Papa working. I wrote to him
every day. When he died, I hanged myself. What
then was there worth keeping?

Dora Maar: *Femme en pleurs,* 1937

D'abord, Picasso didn't make me up, create
me out of clay, or construct me from cutouts.
I was well known for my brains and beauty, for
la photographie, before Éluard introduced us.
My friends—*les Surréalistes:* Man Ray, Breton,
Éluard—could find me at Les Deux Magots
most evenings, playing five-finger filet,
blade aimed between unflinching fingers
on the planked table. Blood would bloom
on the pink roses of my gloves—Picasso
kept those gloves as souvenirs. Picasso—
I always call him that—you don't call
Beethoven "Ludwig," do you?—unless
you are his mother—Picasso turned to Sabartés
and, *en Español,* praised my eyes. But of course,
I grew up in Argentina. When Éluard suggested
a shoot of Picasso working at rue La Boétie,
all fell into place. Though there was always Olga,
flinging abuse, and the other he refused to give up,
Marie-Thérèse. He liked to pit us against each other.
It amused him to paint me in her green-striped blouse,
as if I'd ever wear anything that ugly. *Vraiment,*
he faced two ways, like those in his paintings.
Take his present of Moumoune, part jaguar,
part kitty. I never *liked* cats—well, he knew.
But I had to keep her. She was his gift—
what I liked didn't matter. And those paint
splashes on the wall of my flat that his

pencil transformed into spiders and beetles;
I could not paint them over. At Ménerbes,
the house he gave me as a goodbye offering,
he decorated the toilet seat so I would sit and…
contemplate his genius. (When he moved on
to *la prochaine,* that girl who would give him babies,
he borrowed back the house key for their love nest.
Oh, I hope she enjoyed the resident scorpions!)
Yes, I did what I could to save him. Once, voices
told me his soul was in danger, I told him *kneel down.
Hear what I have to say.* But he had Jacques Lacan
treat me with electroshock therapy. And still,
le cher et beau painted me weeping, over and over.
When he left, *tout le monde* thought I would do
myself in. But I wouldn't give him the satisfaction.

Françoise Gilot: *La femme-fleur*, 1946

He laughed when we met, said I was too pretty
to be a painter. Later, he conceded I had a gift,
urged me to keep working, and invited me to show
him my work from time to time. That's how

it started. Pablo said *In life you toss a ball* ...
With most people, that's all.
But we two? Let's just say we got along.
Although Sabartés predicted it would go wrong.

I belonged in his Blue Period, Pablo would sigh;
he never would have left Montmartre if I ...
Suppose he kept me our little secret, stowed
under the eaves of *les Grands-Augustins*. Who

would know? He would feed me tidbits,
and at night we would explore the streets
like bats. This joke was more than a little real.
Maybe, he laughed, I should wear a djellaba and veil

so no one else's eyes could have me. Still,
for a long time I came and went at will,
while to Marie-Thérèse he commented
on my horsewoman's skill, to torment her,

noted my way with words to torture Dora,
and, well, Olga had already been transformed

to a living shade. I didn't want this foretold fate,
or my dear *grandmère*'s condemnation.

But imagine eating and having the cake,
a banquet with love and art for the taking,
spending afternoons at the Louvre,
studying the diagonals of *Saint Bonaventure*

and discussing the Zurbaràn's resonance—
the ultimate in pure romance.
Enfin, there was nothing to decide. I stayed.
Or rather, I did not go home one day.

But I didn't know what I was in for.
Spanish superstitions, Russian charms,
his own fears held sway.
Nothing could be thrown away.

We'd hold a moment of silence before
going out. A hat on a bed was a curse, what's more,
he believed it bad luck to be prepared—
so I carried Claude to term before Pablo declared

it okay to see a doctor. When the babes cried,
I soothed them, assured Pablo they hadn't died.
He said they were *éléphants, pas enfants!*
He had me right where he wanted.

I'd get up at dawn to build a fire; then at noon
when he woke, he could start right in.
I'd begin his canvases so he could try this
or that course of action. Plus, he'd protest

I was too thin, my bones like a Romanesque
Christ. So, I bided my time like Jeanne d'Arc,
sleeping in armor, while Geneviève Laporte
entertained him for a week or more—

yet he'd swear nothing at all was wrong
and then the next week he'd be gone
to visit the Countess at Perignan.
But before he'd see *me* with another man,

he said he'd rather see me die.
—*go ahead,* he dared, *just try*—
and *No one leaves a man like me.*
Enfin, I decided I needed to be free.

Very well, I said to myself. Just watch.
His friends agreed: I was a bitch.
But he didn't really want me back,
just for his life to keep on track.

I married Luc—our daughter was two—
but I still couldn't shake off Pablo's shadow.

Diane K. Martin

(Maybe that's why Dora Maar swore
only God, after Picasso.) I filed for divorce,

so Claude and Paloma, by his pact,
could have his name. Twelve days after the fact
I read in *Le Monde* his little joke—
he'd already married Jacqueline Roque.

IV

Bag Lady's Song

See, it's a fingernail moon, a waning crescent.
She gets the message. She must return the gloves.
They're elbow-length, lavender, made of kid leather,
borrowed from Helen Mirren. She knows

the streets of the town like fingers on frets,
the chords for the worm in her ear. It's a matter,
she says, of life or breath. The conversation
she's having here (the one in her head) started

fifty-four years ago. She's not lost. She finds his face
on the map. She finds herself on the bench. Her
eyes cloud; she sees a ghost. She points to where
the dog lay dying. It's a matter of focus, she says.

Those mornings: rose petals littered, bees hummed,
a hiss of sprinklers like a hi-hat shimmered.

Magpie Beauty

Even this shiny bit
      taken and repurposed
spark stowed and pocketed
      to be readily at hand
to be caressed and admired
      to have and to keep
in the recesses and crevasses
      privacies and interstices
to husband and to hold
      now especially
when days are short
      the path unspooled
longer than the one wound up
      and the blue moon possessed
of the pearly hours—
      you want its glow
you need its glory
      you require its radiance
it's them or for god's sake you.

Diane K. Martin

Grace

> *The solution to life is death*
> *Yet the question keeps getting asked.*
> —Dean Young

Ever more frequently they're flung
into orbit, like droplets to extremities
by centrifugal force, as if you're the center
of a great washing machine spinning—
a rather solipsistic version of the universe, yes,
old-fashioned wishful thought. Imagining death
is like thinking of not thinking; you are the door
and its closing. Remember that time
the bike flipped and your lights went out?
Of course not. What about those stories
of Sleeping Beauty on the bier waking up
from her nap, the prince who kisses her
the infant she saw yesterday, and the clothing
in her closet very retro? Three deaths, two years,
and Death is just getting started. How many
tears? How many deviled eggs and gladioli?
So far so good. We've made it. That is to say,
we're the ones walking out, playing for time.
As grace goes, it's saving and amazing.

West County Metaphors

Turn the wood-paneled house on its side,
and it's yellowed loose leaf; those evening roses

the gold-illuminated manuscript of a solitary monk.
And the potholes in the street—here we verge

on allegory—are just those days about which mama
warned you. But the dog is herself and not a metaphor,

though she is joy when she wags her tail.

Diane K. Martin

What It Takes

The right boots. Phases of the moon:
waxing gibbous, waning crescent.
Not right before or during her period.
Lined paper, preferably quadrille. Sharp
pencil or fountain pen, black ink.

Fodder, because art needs sustenance:
Egg soft-boiled. Sourdough toast
with peanut butter, crunchy.
Pears and gorgonzola. Red wine,
black coffee, Moroccan mint tea.

Light of early morning (hopeful)
or late afternoon (sentimental). Not
yet the cork-lined room, but one
well appointed, clean. Hum
of mechanism (refrigerator),

organism (bird), companion
(dog tags clinking). Diurnal punctuation—
no midnight sun or long dark hours
of the soul when the street car
commences. Subject poised

at a proper distance: no dead dogs,
sick babies, sons who kill their mothers.
The rules of composition (juxtaposition

of subject and frame) and scale
(union of introspection and outreach).

The slant, the skew, the dip, pitch, lean,
the matter mercurial,
the motley, the mutable,
the various, Protean,
omnifarious, the lucky streak,

good fortune, fair weather, fluke,
halcyon days but not Sargasso seas,
the boom, the bomb, the break,
t's crossed, *i*'s dotted,
prayer spell curse chant benediction.

Diane K. Martin

They Come

In the hour between the dog and the wolf
they come, in single file or chorus, in dactylic
measure, in trochees or in iambs. They come,
they go. I do not stop them, slippery fish
that have tackled rapids, climbed cataracts,
as is their destiny and task. I fall back to the void
of my pillow, and they dissipate. I fall back
to my dreams and my nightmares. But they
have entered, with their muscular music.
They have left their spangled scales.

Life Drawing

Some are born to it,
but you must acquire

that innocence. You want
the dove to whisper

in your ear what the Holy
Ghost of the Christmas

cards told the Virgin
or to turn back to

that green unfurling
that precedes the Word,

unlearning Adam's
naming, returning

to the garden, god
of your own creation.

Diane K. Martin

Ars Poetica

Here's the ode on Vivian Maier,
her insignificant upbringing,
the menial insignificant job—babysitter,

nanny—mother without benefits
—her later (insignificant) life alone,
salvaged by former charges from the street,

and always the Rolleiflex twin-lens extra eye
for shadows, reflections, men in hats,
women in furs, grimy children—

and this: the sidewalk is wet, it's late in the day,
lights are on in the office building.
The man's arm pins the young woman

to the wall. She is angry. I hear him say
she is beautiful when she's angry.
Another couple is walking by.

O women who wove the tapestries,
O Shakespeare's sister,
O *kore* who made and carried Keats's urn.

Soleil Levant: Zabriskie Point

> *each morning, the new baby skin of light*

The landscape a skein unwinding
or a litter of piglets pushing pink teats—
hyperbolic metaphor not equal to
the actual grandeur—meanwhile each moment
the disinterested sun is making it new.

You follow, camera and eye responding,
but what you think is your will is tropism
—this current leaves the self behind,
trumping hunger, denser than desire;
truer north than the pull of iron.

Monet was right: *landscape is impression,*
here nothing exists but that light engenders it,
nothing stays solid as light liquifies.
Or put it this way: the moment is
movement; not sunrise, but sun rising.

Diane K. Martin

Geneviève Laporte: *Le soleil ébloui,* 1951

The young do not understand your painting, I told Picasso.
*Do they understand the song of birds? he asked. The artist must
take your world and shake it, rouse you from your waking sleep.*

It was 1944 when we spoke. We drew lots, at the *lycée,*
to interview *l'artiste,* and it was just my luck. But we kept up
our conversation—across geography and generations—

with letters, postcards, drawings. He sent me books:
the Marquis de Sade, Balzac, St. John of the Cross,
and Tolstoy's *Kreutzer Sonata.* Fast forward seven years:

We first addressed each other as *tu* on a night of thunder
and lightning. Pablo was losing interest in Françoise,
mother of his children—*ça m'était égal.* We had something

different—yet the day after Françoise left with his children,
he had his car come round to take me to Vallauris. *First,
change the sheets,* I told him. Don't ask me why I said that.

Sylvette David: *Portrait de Sylvette,* 1954

My profile and blonde ponytail,
just a bland and simple tale.

Diane K. Martin

Jacqueline Roque: *Femme nue au bonnet turc,* 1955

I made myself useful. *C'est tout.* I made sure
he took his medicines, drank his hot tisane,
sipped the carrot-and-pea soup I prepared
without pepper. I waited outside his studio
in case he wanted for anything. The Gilot
woman used her children as excuse to come
back whenever she wanted. It was most
disruptive, like that time at Vallauris when she
rode her horse at the *corrida* in his honor.
You would think she could see *c'était ridicule.*
After that I made it my job to keep them
away from *Monseigneur.* They all wanted
something: dealers, journalists, riffraff, his children ...

But every woman for twenty years was Jacqueline.
This face, this body—Nude in a Turkish Hat,
Woman in Algiers.... He was the sun I faced all day,
at night, the moon. I watched him create; I never
turned away—paintings, etchings, sculptures in clay—
seven days a week. God Himself only worked six.

Muse Rebellion

Because seven people sat in a bar,
agreeably disagreeing about Art,
she hovered, a spirit like vermouth
in a martini, in the purple light
some feet above the table.

But she was sick of being slave
(*White Goddess* really!), commanded
to appear, breathe the right words in his ear
in the right order or resuscitate him
lip to lip until the susurrus evoked

the perfect-pitch vibrato of his heart.
All those years chasing enlightenment
and yet another saint or angel, charming
the hand scraping palettes, groping chiaroscuro
grottoes, pointing toward the vanishing point.

Didn't they know without her they'd have
only their science and their cynicism? Arriving
at the moon, they'd forget why they ever went.
Descending to the ocean floor they'd
find it neither pearled nor profound.

She'd heard it all before: *Neoclassic-impressionist-surrealist-pop, dada-metaphysical-jazz-funk-bop, fusion, expressionist, conceptual, rock,*

Diane K. Martin

imagist, modern, post-, hip hop—
she wanted very much to lie down.

What She Meant

when she said that she wanted nothing
was not sainthood or self-abnegation
or that her eyes were fixed on the prize

of love. Perhaps she had an inkling
of his leaving, a foreshadowing of frozen
footsteps, a preview of the conversation

where he said he'd take the China blue rug
and half of everything. *Take the whole heart*
she should have said, as for Solomon.

But the world is stuff. How could she not want
to make an entrance in the red dress,
run her hands through plum silks

and gauzy linens, collect the model life,
like a dollhouse, with its mini drapes,
itsy-bitsy chairs, teensy cradle?

How could she not want all things
that shimmer, hum, and glitter?
Just one could never be enough. So

she said *nothing*—though when she clutches
the comforter that last time, she'll plead
as Goethe did for light: *more, give me more.*

Diane K. Martin

Will's Will

Gather up new-fallen words,
compact, and throw. You
want the bull's-eye but also
the glow that each bean seed
underground must know,
magnanimous sun confirming
its singularity. Allow it's
hard to tell what will last
of the dead: some words
you wrote they'll remember
you by, a few quid for the kids,
and for the one you wed,
your second-best bed.

Gertrude Said Matisse's Pears

sat in a blue bowl in winter light.
The painter's overcoat was thin;
the gloves were fingerless. The stove

stayed cold although wind prised
the cracked glass. Matisse
worked fast—as juice oozed

from bruised pears. His brush
transmuted curves to flat canvas;
the fruit had the scent of time.

Diane K. Martin

Take 5

Fall
into a deep well, every bone broken,
from which only your voice can rise

Scour
your body with blue snow
under a waxing gibbous moon

Listen
to the slow suction
of snail across the window

Cleanse
milk spill on the desk
—a streak of sun

Be
in clear shallow water—
smooth stones, small mud-colored fish

Shutting the Door

behind which lurks prince or tiger,
equally dangerous. We are meat

for both, me and my conjoined twin,
who wears her heart outside her body,

slung beneath the shoulder
so easy to grab, bite, break.

So we are keen to let the door stay
latched and fastened with a chain

though who's to say if what
shields us also locks us in.

Notes

"In the mouth of the wolf" is an Italian expression used in opera and theatre to wish a performer good luck.

"*Excusez-moi de vous déranger*" means "sorry to disturb you."

Pattern for "Hue and Cry" (poem) adapted from "Shine," by Sylvia Curbelo.

Tessitura is the most comfortable range for a given voice.

The term *White Goddess* was used by Robert Graves, in his book *The White Goddess: a Historical Grammar of Poetic Myth*, (press, 1948).

Acknowledgments

During a residency at Vermont Studio Center in the early 2000s, fed up with writing about myself and intrigued by the idea of artistic genius, I started reading about Pablo Picasso (VSC, much thanks for the inspiration and time in your library).

I became fascinated by Picasso and then by the women in his life. I began populating poems with these women, taking on their personas. Later, Robert Hass, discussing these poems with me, suggested that this was a book about women and art (thank you, Bob).

Some of the books I read at Vermont Studio Center—and later—include *Loving Picasso: The Private Journal of Fernande Olivier; Life With Picasso,* by Françoise Gilot and Carlton Lake; *Picasso: Creator and Destroyer,* by Arianna Stassinopoulos Huffington and Wanda McCaddon; several volumes of the John Richardson biographies; and *Picasso,* by Gertrude Stein. My apologies that a complete list of the books I drew on for inspiration is impossible to reconstruct. My Picasso women poems, while true in spirit, are not intended as historical or wholly biographical documents.

And although this book started with women and art, it continues exploring creativity itself, addressing perspective, darkness and light, and the art of living a life.

I need to express my gratitude to Michael Wiegers and *Narrative Magazine* for publishing the twelve Picasso poems, now in each section of *Hue & Cry,* and also to *A Face to Meet the Faces* anthology, which published "Fernande Olivier: *Femme dormante (Meditation),* 1904." Titles and poems may have since been revised.

Thank you to David Dodd Lee and to April Ossmann, each of whom read different early versions of *Hue & Cry;* their suggestions helped crystallize this book.

Much gratitude to Eduardo Corral for his friendship, support, and generous words. Thanks, also, to David Young and to Erin Belieu for the honor of their praise.

Thank you to my friends in Thirteen Ways, my old poetry group (you know who you are).

I am grateful for support and time at Bread Loaf Writers Conference, Virginia Center for the Creative Arts, Napa Valley Writers Conference, Prague Summer Program for Writers, and the Community of Writers at Squaw Valley, in addition to Vermont Studio Center.

Thank you, thank you, thank you to my friend, the wonderful poet Robert Thomas, who read everything here many times over. I would not have made it without your encouragement.

And a heart full of gratitude to John F. Martin, my husband, for your support and for sharing this life of love and art. Thanks, also, to our son Nathaniel.

Thank you to the following publications for publishing the poems in *Hue & Cry,* some of which have been revised since and given different titles:

The Awl: "Shutting the Door"

Bellingham Review: "Shocking the Well"

A Bird Black as the Sun, eds. Enid Osborn & Cynthia Anderson (Green Poet Press, 2011): "Bird Through Frames"

B O D Y: "Magpie Beauty"

Boxcar: "Angle of Incidence"

Cimarron Review: "At the Origin of the World"

Connotation Press: "*La Vie (en Rose),*" "The Party," "Take 5," and "Self-Help Dream of a Yellow Canvas" (in A Poetry Congeries)

Crab Creek Review: "Plot," "Silent Night"

CutBank: "Bomb" and "*Soleil Levant:* Zabriskie Point"

Cutthroat Magazine: "Cold Music," "Night Mind," "Radio Frequency," and "Red Herring"

DIAGRAM: "Earthquake Weather"

Diode: "Will's Will"

A Face to Meet the Faces, eds. Stacey Lynn Brown & Oliver de la Paz (University of Akron Press, 2012): "Fernande Olivier: Femme dormante (Meditation), 1904"

FIELD: "Refract" and "Muse Rebellion"

Global Geneva: "In the Mouth of the Wolf"

Harvard Review: "A Study in Chiaroscuro"

Kenyon Review: "*Excusez-moi de vous déranger*"

Narrative Magazine: "Demoiselle" (12 poems)

North American Review: "Indelible"

Painted Bride: "One Question"

Rhino: "Fata Morgana"

Smartish Pace (Erskine J. Poetry Prize): "Hue and Cry"

Summerset: "Gertrude Said Matisse's Pears"

SWWIM: "Piece of Work"

Tar River Review: "MacGuffin"

Tinderbox: "What She Meant"

Valparaiso Poetry Review: "Life Drawing"

Waccamaw: "What It Takes"

Women's Voices for Change: "Ars Poetica"

Zócalo Public Square: "POV"

ZYZZYVA: "Grace"

About the Author

Born in the Bronx, **Diane K. Martin** grew up in Yonkers, New York. She has a BA in English from the University of Rochester and a Master's in English with a Concentration in Creative Writing from San Francisco State University. Her work has appeared in *American Poetry Review, Field, Harvard Review, Kenyon Review, New England Review, Plume, Tin House, Zyzzyva,* and many other journals and anthologies, including *Best New Poets*. One of her poems received a Pushcart Special Mention, and the title poem of this manuscript won the poetry prize from *Smartish Pace*. In addition, in 2004, her work was awarded second place in the *Nimrod*/Hardman Pablo Neruda Prize judged by B. H. Fairchild. Her collection *Conjugated Visits,* a National Poetry Series finalist, was published in 2010 by Dream Horse Press. After 36 years in San Francisco, Diane now lives in western Sonoma County, where she teaches Grammar, Mechanics, and Usage for Editors for UC Berkeley Extension online and also gardens and walks her dog.

www.ingramcontent.com/pod-product-compliance
Lightning Source LLC
Chambersburg PA
CBHW020336170426
43200CB00006B/404